BATS!

Written by Roger Generazzo
Illustrated by Greg Harris
Reviewed by Dr. Edward M. Spevak,
Assistant Curator of Mammals at the Bronx Zoo.

© 2000 McClanahan Book Company, Inc.
All rights reserved.
Published by McClanahan Book Company, Inc.
23 West 26th Street, New York, NY 10010
ISBN: 0-7681-0209-X
Printed in the U.S.A.
10 9 8 7 6 5 4 3 2 1

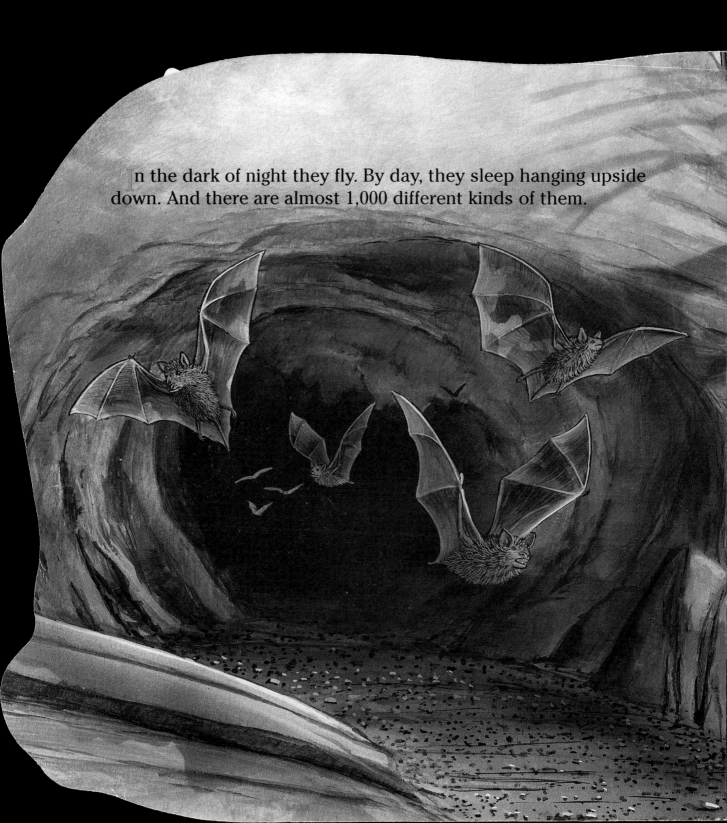

n the dark of night they fly. By day, they sleep hanging upside down. And there are almost 1,000 different kinds of them.

What are they?
(Turn the page to find out. . .)

Answer: BATS!

For centuries, people thought bats were evil creatures that drank blood and carried sickness. While a few kinds of bats do drink the blood of large animals such as cattle and can carry diseases such as rabies, bats rarely harm people.

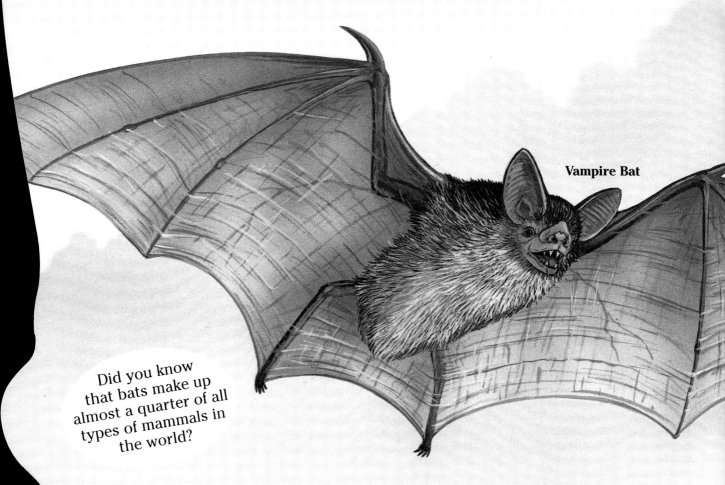

Vampire Bat

Did you know that bats make up almost a quarter of all types of mammals in the world?

What is a bat?

Like dogs and cats, bats belong to a group of animals called **mammals**. Like all mammal mothers, bat moms feed their babies milk.

Scientists divide bats into two main groups—**megabats** and **microbats**. Megabats are usually larger than microbats, and they have better eyesight.

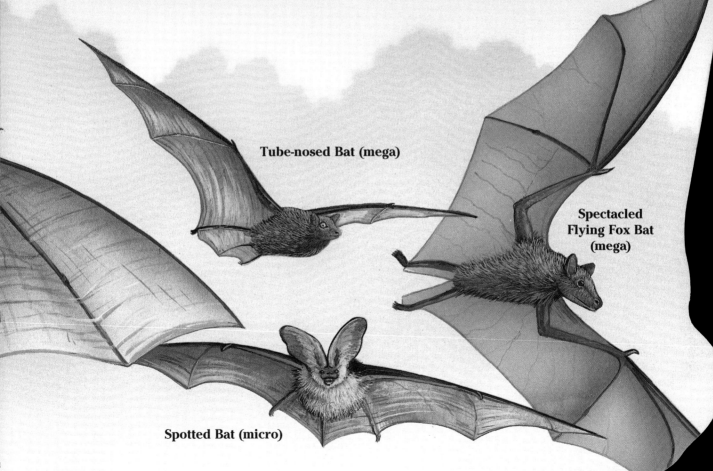

Tube-nosed Bat (mega)

Spectacled Flying Fox Bat (mega)

Spotted Bat (micro)

The bat is the only kind of mammal that can fly. In fact, some bats can only fly—they cannot walk! A bat's wings are made of thin skin that's attached to its furry body and feet. Each wing includes five fingers, one of which is a claw. The bat's feet also have toes with claws. All of these claws help the bat hold onto rocks and branches.

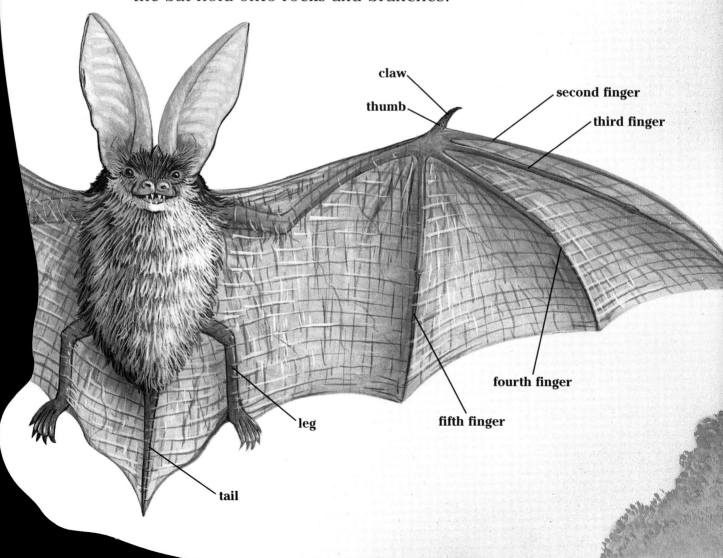

claw

thumb

second finger

third finger

fourth finger

fifth finger

leg

tail

From tip to tip, some kinds of bats, like Giant Flying Foxes, have a wingspan as wide as 6 feet (2 m). But there are also tiny bats, like Bumblebee Bats, with wingspans of only 6 inches (15 cm)—smaller than the length of a new pencil. Bats may weigh less than a penny. Or they can weigh as much as 2.2 pounds (1 kg)—the weight of a 700-page book!

Did you know that the Bumblebee Bat is the smallest mammal in the world?

Giant Flying Fox

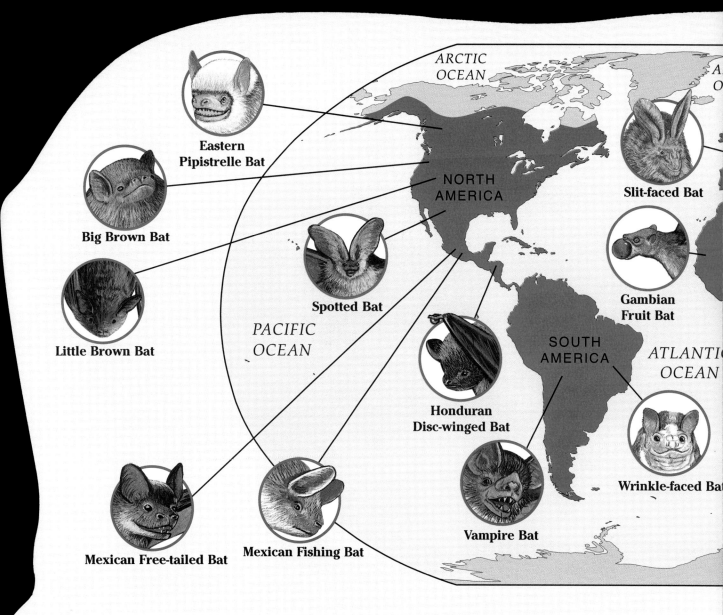

ARCTIC OCEAN

A...
O...

Eastern Pipistrelle Bat

Slit-faced Bat

NORTH AMERICA

Big Brown Bat

Gambian Fruit Bat

Spotted Bat

Little Brown Bat

PACIFIC OCEAN

SOUTH AMERICA

ATLANTI... OCEAN

Honduran Disc-winged Bat

Wrinkle-faced Bat

Vampire Bat

Mexican Free-tailed Bat

Mexican Fishing Bat

Bats live all over the world, except in places that are always cold. But no matter where they live, bats are **nocturnal**—that means they move about and search for food mostly at night. During the day, they groom themselves, care for their young, and sleep.

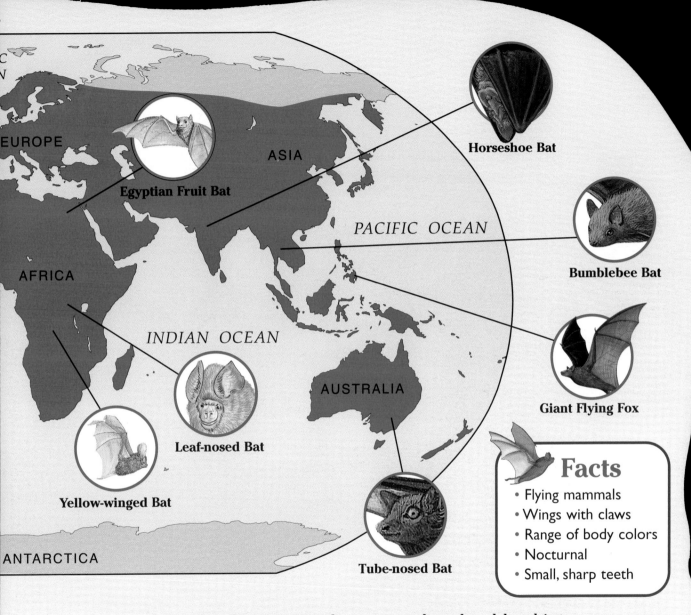

EUROPE

ASIA

Horseshoe Bat

Egyptian Fruit Bat

PACIFIC OCEAN

Bumblebee Bat

AFRICA

INDIAN OCEAN

AUSTRALIA

Giant Flying Fox

Leaf-nosed Bat

Yellow-winged Bat

Facts
• Flying mammals
• Wings with claws
• Range of body colors
• Nocturnal
• Small, sharp teeth

ANTARCTICA

Tube-nosed Bat

Like many timid creatures, bats are colored to blend into their surroundings. Tropical bats that live in the jungle may be brightly colored. Bats that live in colder climates tend to be black, brown, or gray. One other interesting fact about bat bodies: they have very sharp little teeth...

What do bats eat?

Megabats usually eat fruits and flower nectar. Such food is plentiful in the tropics of Africa and Asia where they live.

Gambian Fruit Bat

Microbats, on the other hand, feed mostly on insects, spiders, and scorpions. Many of these bats catch insects in their mouths or wings as they fly. A few microbats eat frogs, lizards, and fish. And vampire bats, with their razor sharp teeth, drink animal blood!

A single brown bat can catch and eat 1200 mosquitoes in just one hour.

Brown Bat

How do bats find food?

Megabats use their very sharp eyesight and a good sense of smell to find food. They even see well at night. The expression "blind as a bat" doesn't refer to megabats!

Mexican Fishing Bat

Most microbats don't have good eyesight. They use a process called **echolocation** to find meals. The microbat sends out a high-pitched sound through its mouth or nose—so high that people can't even hear it. The sound bounces off nearby objects and comes back to the bat as echoes. From the echoes, the bat knows what the object is, where it is, and how fast it is moving!

Mexican fishing bats use echolocation to find a minnow's fin that is only a fraction of an inch (1 cm) above a pond's surface!

Where do bats live?

Similar kinds of bats live in groups called **colonies**. The place where the colony lives together is called a **roost**. Bats may use different roosts during the night—to rest, to eat, and to find shelter.

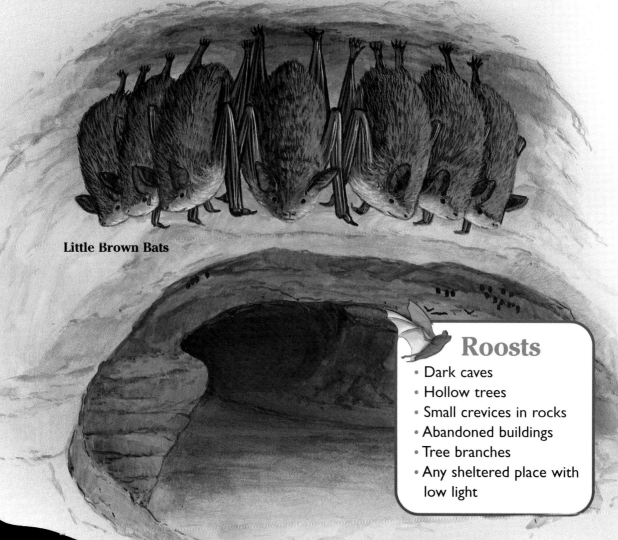

Little Brown Bats

Roosts

- Dark caves
- Hollow trees
- Small crevices in rocks
- Abandoned buildings
- Tree branches
- Any sheltered place with low light

When sleeping in their roosts, bats hang upside down. The claws on their feet and wings help them hold on to cave ceilings, branches, and other high places.

Lyle's
Flying Foxes

In India, one kind of horseshoe bat shares the roost with large porcupines. Ouch!

Disc-winged Bat

How does a bat grow up?

Every spring, mother bats give birth in nursery caves. When the mother leaves the cave roost to find food, she usually goes without her baby, which is called a **pup**. Her waiting pup may play with other pups along the walls or on the floor of the roost. When the mother returns, she finds her baby by its smell and the sounds it makes—even when there are thousands of other babies in the roost!

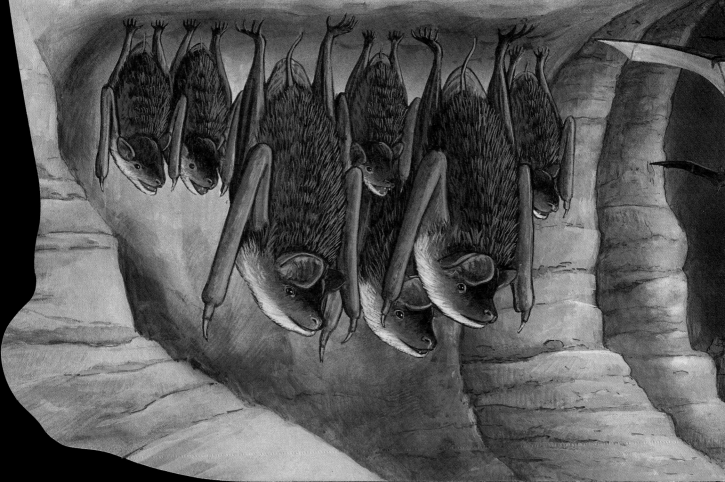

The pups grow up very fast, usually taking their first flight when they are three weeks old. Each pup continues to drink its mother's milk for six weeks. Within a couple of months, it learns how to fly out into the dark night with its mother to find food.

Most bat females have only one **pup** each year.

Mexican Free-tailed Bats

What happens to bats in the winter?

Some bats that live in places where the winter temperature goes below freezing **migrate**. That means they fly to a place where the weather is warmer. It's like taking a vacation in the tropics!

Mexican Free-tailed Bats

Mexican free-tailed bats migrate almost a thousand miles (1600 km) from the southwestern United States to central Mexico.

Other bats stay through the cold winter. But they gather in roosts to sleep or **hibernate** until warmer weather returns because there is less food to eat in winter. Bats that live in places where the weather is always warm don't have to migrate or hibernate.

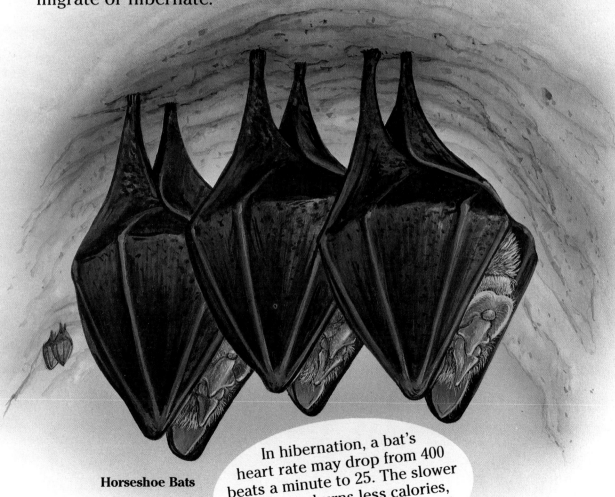

Horseshoe Bats

In hibernation, a bat's heart rate may drop from 400 beats a minute to 25. The slower heart rate burns less calories, so the bat can go without food for a long time.

How do bats protect themselves?

Bats are protected from most animals because they fly at night when other creatures are asleep. Also, bats live in isolated roosts, hanging from high places, where animals can't get to them. Bats have few enemies—mainly hawks, owls, and snakes.

Sometimes people become a bat's worst enemy because they fear it. But people are only in danger if they pick up a sick bat. The animal may bite in self-defense.

Because they have few enemies, many bats live a long time. Some have been known to live for more than 30 years! The little brown bat is the world's longest-lived mammal for its small size, with a life-span of more than 32 years!

Bet you didn't know . . .

The pallid bat is immune to the stings of scorpions and centipedes, which it eats.

The big brown bat of Eastern North America usually gives birth to twins.

The vampire bat drinks a little less than a thimbleful of blood each night.

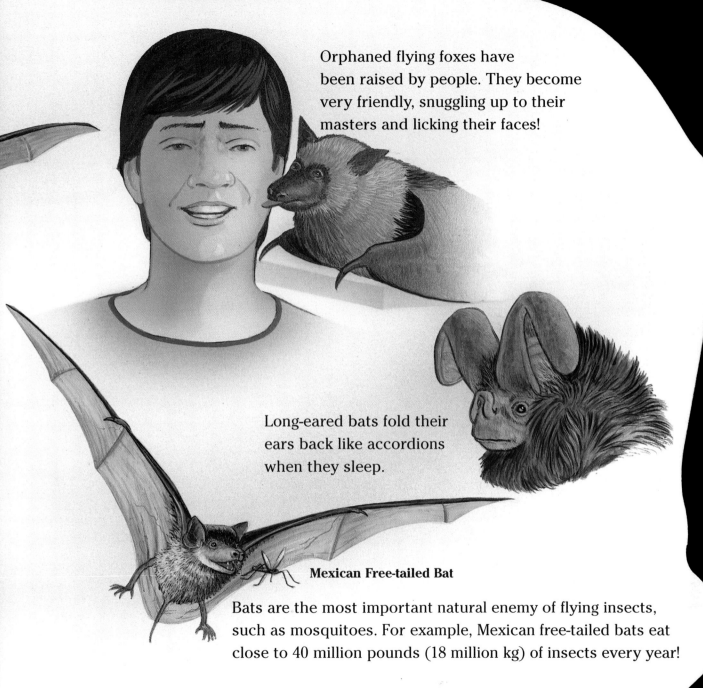

Orphaned flying foxes have been raised by people. They become very friendly, snuggling up to their masters and licking their faces!

Long-eared bats fold their ears back like accordions when they sleep.

Mexican Free-tailed Bat

Bats are the most important natural enemy of flying insects, such as mosquitoes. For example, Mexican free-tailed bats eat close to 40 million pounds (18 million kg) of insects every year!

Yes, indeed, bats are fascinating...

and if you're lucky enough to live near a cave or forest, you may look up one evening just before dark and catch a glimpse of this marvel of the air—the only mammal that flies!